Encounters with God

The First and Second
Epistles of PETER

Encounters with God

The First and Second Epistles of PETER

Published in Nashville, Tennessee, by Thomas Nelson. Thomas Nelson is a registered trademark of Thomas Nelson, Inc.

Thomas Nelson, Inc. titles may be purchased in bulk for educational, business, fund-raising, or sales promotional use. For information, please e-mail SpecialMarkets@ThomasNelson.com.

ISBN 978-1-4185-2654-2

Printed in the United States of America

HB 11.30.2023

CONTENTS

AN INTRODUCTION TO THE FIRST AND SECOND EPISTLES OF PETER

This study guide covers the first and second epistles of Peter. These letters were written to believers who were under or were facing the likelihood of severe persecution. Few people in the western world today can fathom the horrors of the persecution these early believers experienced or the fear associated with persecution.

Tacitus, a second century Roman historian who disliked Christians, recorded that Nero burned Christians alive to light his gardens and that he fed Christians to wild animals for entertainment. Christians were routinely slandered, defamed, boycotted, mobbed, imprisoned, and killed because of their faith. Public suspicion and antagonism escalated throughout the first century. In many sectors of the Roman Empire, Christians were regarded as treacherous traitors because they believed in a future King, Jesus the Christ, who would someday return to earth to establish worldwide rule. This idea not only made Rome's rulers nervous, but also caused the general populace to regard Christians as a potential menace to their security and financial prosperity.

After AD 64 many sectors of the Roman Empire considered it a criminal offense to bear the name of Christ. One historian noted that Christians were slaughtered with public approval for the crime of allegedly promoting "hatred of the human race." Both the apostle Paul and the apostle Peter were killed in Rome for their faith during this period of intense persecution of the mid to latter half of the first century.

The first letter of Peter was addressed to the "pilgrims of the Dispersion" (1 Pet. 1:1). This common designation was applied to Jewish Christians who had been scattered by persecution throughout the Roman Empire. Peter also applied the term to converted Gentiles who had suffered persecution (1 Pet. 2:9–10). The letter was intended to be circulated among bodies of believers in Pontus, Galatia, Cappadocia, Asia, and Bithynia, the region now known as Turkey. The first letter presents encouragement and assurance that the believers have an eternal inheritance made possible by the precious shed blood of Christ. They are exhorted to live holy lives, individually and corporately in the church, and they are given practical instruction about how to respond to persecution with holy living in the community, in the workplace, and in marriage. Peter called for the community of faith to exhibit irreproachable integrity and to accept any form of suffering on Christ's behalf as a great honor. Peter admonished them to return good for evil, and to trust God for justice. Peter's promise to the believers remains applicable to believers of all generations: stay obedient despite persecution, and God will reward you according to your faithfulness.

In the second letter Peter reinforced many of the themes of the first letter, but he appears to have written more personally to his audience. Besides being a general letter, the epistle has overtones of being a testament letter, giving final instructions from a dying father or leader. Peter wrote to those who were facing persecution from outside the church and heretical teachings within the church. Peter challenged those of faith to grow in their faith, remain firm in their stance against false doctrines and prepare for the Day of the Lord. He also stressed patience, simultaneously warning those who tried to lead God's people astray, live immoral lives, or preach empty or false doctrines. His message has been one of tremendous hope and encouragement to believers through the ages: God is in control and will bring all things to completion according to His timetable.

Both letters were likely written between AD 62 and 67, after Paul was martyred and before Nero was removed from power. Bible scholars generally believe Peter was martyred during the Neronian persecutions (AD 64–68), likely in AD 67. Legend claims that Peter felt unworthy to be crucified as Jesus had been and that he begged his executioner to crucify him upside down.

About the Author, Peter. Peter, an apostle of Jesus and an eyewitness to the transfiguration (2 Pet. 1:1–17; Matt. 17:1–13) is generally accepted as the author of both letters, although for centuries, his authorship was questioned for several reasons.

First, a number of people who were influenced by Peter and who knew of Peter's popularity appear to have written treatises and letters in Peter's name, either to convey to others what they had heard preached by Peter or to align themselves with Peter's authority and prominence in the early church. These two letters, however, stand apart from other letters in their direct claim to spiritual authority granted to an apostle.

Second, some have argued that the sophisticated literary style of 1 Peter was not likely to have been the work of an "uneducated and untrained" Galilean fisherman such as Peter (Acts 4:13). The truth, however, is that

Peter, by vocation, was a successful businessman in a bilingual region of Galilee, and he very likely was fluent in both Aramaic and Greek. He also may have used Silvanus as an amanuensis or secretary to record or polish his message, including 1 Peter (1 Pet. 5:12). Furthermore, after thirty years of preaching and teaching the gospel, Peter very likely had acquired a more polished style of writing and speaking than seems to be presented in the Gospels.

Third, some have contended that the letters were actually written by Paul since they present teachings that are similar to Paul's letters. An affinity to Paul's doctrines is perhaps the outgrowth of their friendship and discussion on the true nature of the gospel. A close examination of the letters makes it clear that the letters attributed to Peter have a different voice and style.

Fourth, a number of scholars have questioned whether *both* 1 and 2 Peter were written by Peter. They cite a different style and vocabulary in the second letter as well as some difference in subject matter. They also note that 2 Peter is very similar to the book of Jude and that a number of early church leaders did not include 2 Peter in their list of authentic writings— Eusebias (AD 265–340) even went so far as to refer to it as a "disputed writing." On the other hand, both ancient and modern biblical scholars have noted that no other biblical book is as similar to I Peter. They also note that Peter and Jude likely were acquainted or were familiar with each other's writings and teachings. Still others have noted that the differences in style may have been a matter of whether Peter used a secretary in writing the second letter. The second letter very likely was written after Peter's imprisonment and shortly before his death, in which case the services of a skilled secretary were likely not available to him. Although there are differences in style, the two letters also have amazing similarities. Both use common Hebrew expressions, exhibit a unique style of verbal repetition, and include words used nowhere else in the New Testament. While some of the early church leaders may have questioned whether Peter wrote the second letter, other early church leaders widely supported the position that he did write the letter. Origen, an early church leader writing at the beginning of the third century, quoted from the letter six times. By the fourth century, church councils had fully accepted the second letter as an authentic writing of Peter.

Peter was one of Jesus' closest apostles, always named first in any list of the apostles. He routinely was present with James and John at a number of pivotal events. Peter was the first of the apostles to declare that Jesus was the Christ. He is the apostle who answered Jesus' call and walked on water, was present when Jesus raised the daughter of Jairus from her deathbed, was called to a nearby position of prayer in the Garden of Gethsemane, and raced to the empty tomb with John. It was Peter who, after denying Jesus three times, received full forgiveness from Jesus and was given a three-fold commission for ministry. It was Peter who preached powerfully on the Day of Pentecost and who became a beloved leader of the early church—first in Jerusalem, and later to the Gentiles at the house of Cornelius. Peter very likely had strong influence on Mark as Mark wrote his Gospel account.

Little is known of Peter's ministry in later years. He may have traveled among the churches in Asia Minor since they are the recipients of his letters. Church tradition also states that he traveled to Rome and died there. Rome was referred to in code as "Babylon" among the early Christians (1 Pet. 5:13).

Peter was recognized by Jesus and by those in the early church as having a heart of ready obedience, a remarkable faith, and depth of spiritual insight. Yet he also appears to have struggled with *self* and with a quick temper. His life is an example to all believers that anyone can find forgiveness, be filled with the Spirit, and make a significant contribution to God's kingdom.

AN OVERVIEW OF OUR STUDY OF THE FIRST AND SECOND EPISTLES OF PETER

This study guide presents seven lessons drawn from the first and second epistles of Peter. It elaborates upon the commentary included in the *Blackaby Study Bible*:

Lesson #1: Recipients of a Heavenly Inheritance

Lesson #2: Tested by Fiery Trials

Lesson #3: Living and Precious Stones

Lesson #4: Partakers of the Divine Nature

Lesson #5: Remaining Steadfast in the Light

Lesson #6: Rejecting False Teaching

Lesson #7: Looking for Christ's Coming

Personal or Group Use. These lessons are offered for personal study and reflection or for small-group Bible study. The study questions asked may be answered by an individual reader or used as a foundation for group discussion. A segment titled "Notes to Leaders of Small Groups" is included at the back of this book to help those leading a group study of this material.

Before you embark on this study, we encourage you to read in full the statement in the *Blackaby Study Bible* titled "How to Study the Bible." Our contention is always that the Bible is unique among all literature. It is God's definitive word for humanity. The Bible is

- *inspired*—"God-breathed"

- *authoritative*—absolutely the final word on any spiritual matter

- *the plumb line of truth*—the standard against which all human activity and reasoning must be evaluated

The Bible is fascinating in that it has remarkable diversity but also remarkable unity. Its books were penned by a diverse assortment of authors representing a variety of languages and cultures, and it contains a number of literary forms. But the Bible's message from cover to cover is clear, consistent, and unified.

More than mere words on a page, the Bible is an encounter with God Himself. No book is more critical to your life. The very essence of the Bible is the Lord Himself.

The Holy Spirit speaks through the Bible. He also communicates during your time of prayer, in your life circumstances, and through the church. Read your Bible in an attitude of prayer, and allow the Holy Spirit to make you aware of God's activity in and through your personal life. Write down what you learn, meditate on it, and adjust your thoughts, attitudes, and behavior accordingly. Look for ways every day to apply the truth of God's Word to your circumstances and relationships. God is not random; He is orderly and intentional in the way He speaks to you.

Be encouraged—the Bible is *not* too difficult for the average person to understand if that person asks the Holy Spirit for help. (Furthermore, not even the most brilliant person can fully understand the Bible apart from the Holy Spirit's help!) God desires for you to know Him and to know His Word. Every person who reads the Bible can learn from it. The person who will receive *maximum* benefits from reading and studying the Bible, however, is the person who:

- *is born again* (John 3:35). Those who are born again and have received the gift of His Spirit have a distinct advantage in understanding the deeper truths of God's Word.

- *has a heart that desires to learn God's truth.* Your attitude greatly influences the outcome of Bible study. Resist the temptation to focus on what others have said about the Bible. Allow the Holy Spirit to guide you as you study God's Word for yourself.

- *has a heart that seeks to obey God.* The Holy Spirit teaches the most to those who desire to apply what they learn.

Begin your Bible study with prayer, asking the Holy Spirit to guide your thoughts and to impress upon you what is on God's heart. Then make plans to adjust your life immediately to obey the Lord fully.

As you read and study the Bible, your purpose is not to *create* meaning, but to *discover* the meaning of the text with the Holy Spirit's guidance. Ask yourself, "What did the author have in mind? How was this applied by those who first heard these words?" Especially in your study of Paul's letters, look for ways in which the truths can be applied directly to your personal, practical, daily Christian walk and to the life of your church.

At times you may find it helpful to consult other passages of the Bible (made available in the center columns in the *Blackaby Study Bible*), or the commentary that is in the margins of the *Blackaby Study Bible*.

Keep in mind always that Bible study is not primarily an exercise for acquiring information but an opportunity for transformation. Bible study is your opportunity to encounter God and to be changed in His presence. When God speaks to your heart, nothing remains the same. Jesus said, "He who has ears to hear, let him hear" (Matt. 13:9). Choose to have ears that desire to hear!

The B-A-S-I-Cs of Each Study in This Guide. Each lesson in this study guide has five segments, using the word BASIC as an acronym. The word BASIC does not allude to elementary or simple, but rather to foundational. These studies extend the concepts that are part of the *Blackaby Study Bible* commentary and are focused on key aspects of what it means to be a Christ-follower in today's world. The BASIC acronym stands for:

> *B = Bible Focus.* This segment presents the central passage for the lesson
> · and a general explanation that covers the central theme or concern.

> *A = Application for Today.* This segment has a story or illustration related to current-day events with questions that link the Bible text to today's issues, problems, and concerns.

> *S = Supplementary Scriptures to Consider.* In this segment other Bible verses related to the general theme of the lesson are explored.

> *I = Introspection and Implications.* In this segment questions are asked that lead to deeper reflection about one's personal faith journey and life experiences.

> *C = Communicating the Good News.* In this segment challenging questions point to ways the lesson's truth might be lived out and shared with others, whether to win the lost or build up the church.

Lesson #1

RECIPIENTS OF A HEAVENLY INHERITANCE

Inheritance: the wealth, property, or title of an ancestor, received when the ancestor dies

B
Bible Focus

> Blessed be the God and Father of our Lord Jesus Christ,
> who according to His abundant mercy has begotten us again
> to a living hope through the resurrection of Jesus Christ from
> the dead, to an inheritance incorruptible and undefiled and
> that does not fade away, reserved in heaven for you, who are
> kept by the power of God through faith for salvation ready to
> be revealed in the last time. . . .
>
> Of this salvation the prophets have inquired and searched
> carefully, who prophesied of the grace that would come to you,
> searching what, or what manner of time, the Spirit of Christ
> who was in them was indicating when He testified beforehand
> the sufferings of Christ and the glories that would follow. To
> them it was revealed that, not to themselves, but to us they
> were ministering the things which now have been reported to
> you through those who have preached the gospel to you by the
> Holy Spirit sent from heaven—things which angels desire to
> look into (1 Pet. 1:3–5, 10–12).

In all of the New Testament there are few passages that present more of the great fundamental Christian ideas in so few words. The passage begins with a doxology—a praise statement to God. This statement, however, is distinctly different from the traditional doxology of the Jews: "Blessed art thou, O God." The Christian doxology addresses God as Father of the Lord Jesus Christ. Peter did not offer praise to a distant, unknown God, but to a God who can be identified and readily approached.

The phrase "begotten us again" refers to spiritual rebirth or what many Christians today call being "born again" or "the salvation experience." Peter made several strong statements about what it means to be spiritually reborn:

- *spiritual rebirth is an act of God, according to His will.* It is not achieved by man. Rather, it is the work of the Spirit as a person yields himself to the Spirit.

- *spiritual rebirth happens through the creative word of God in Jesus Christ* (1 Pet. 1:23). Those who hear the good news of Jesus' atoning sacrifice, and believe He is the Son of God who died for the sins of mankind, are enabled to believe and receive by faith a newness of life.

- *the spiritually reborn person has a "living hope," which has the Resurrection of Christ Jesus as its evidence.* The Christian is linked to eternal life because the spiritual rebirth is something created from incorruptible seed—it is from the eternal realm of the Spirit.

- *the spiritually reborn person enters into a great inheritance.* The word used here in the Greek, *kleronomia*, is a word used regularly in the Greek Old Testament for the inheritance of Canaan as the promised land. This type of inheritance refers to something that will certainly be possessed *fully* in the future.

Peter noted that the inheritance of the Christian is imperishable: it cannot be taken over by any invading army. It is also undefilable: it cannot be polluted by the surrounding society. And, it is unfading: the joy of it does not diminish over time. These three attributes of the inheritance had special meaning to the early church as it faced persecution. Nothing, Peter declared to them, can destroy what Christ has secured for you, not even the full power of Rome. Nothing can defile you, no matter how hideous a death you may face for your faith. Heaven declares you clean. Nothing can take away your joy unless you allow it to do so.

To more fully grasp what Peter was saying, consider what the lost person does *not* have.

The unsaved sinner does *not* have forgiveness of sin, does *not* have a real hope of eternal *life* after death, does *not* have the abiding and regenerating power of the Holy Spirit, and does *not* have the certain hope of heavenly inheritance. The unsaved person is prone to the whims of the age in which he lives and the vagrancies of the culture around him. He is readily polluted in his thinking and emotions by the sins prevalent in his society. He has only fleeting happiness rather than a wellspring of unending joy.

The prophets longed for spiritual rebirth, Peter declared. The angels are mystified by it and would like to know more about it. There is no higher privilege than to have heard the gospel message, believed it, and received Jesus as Savior. There is no greater joy than to follow Him as Lord.

Nothing is as amazing as spiritual rebirth! We must never take it for granted. We must never cease to give it highest value!

A
Application for Today

"Do you have a relationship with Jesus Christ?" a woman rather matter-of-factly asked a coworker with whom she was dining at a restaurant. Both women worked as analysts for an investments brokerage firm in a large city. The two had been discussing the importance of having meaningful relationships in one's life and how difficult such relationships were to achieve in a large fast-paced city and in a lifestyle that, for them at least, seemed highly work-oriented. The transition to bringing up a *relationship* with Jesus had seemed a natural extension of that topic.

"Oh, there's nothing in religion for me," her coworker said.

"I didn't say religion," the woman replied. "I don't consider myself to be extremely religious. I was just curious as to whether you have a relationship with Jesus Christ."

"I doubt there's anything in that for me, either," replied the coworker with a tinge of sarcasm to her voice.

"I once thought that," the woman said, "but then I established a relationship with Jesus, and it has turned out to be the most satisfying and meaningful relationship I've ever had."

The coworker was silent.

"I realize you probably think I'm trying to cram my faith down your throat," the woman said, "but I'm not. We've been talking about relationships and how they are a matter of giving and receiving. Given our jobs in the brokerage business, we have been using terms like 'return on investment.' Well, my relationship with Jesus is the relationship that has given me the greatest 'return on investment' I've ever received."

"How so?" the coworker asked.

The woman replied: "I invested simple and sincere belief that Jesus is the Son of God who died for my sins. I asked God to forgive the sins that had been standing between us and to establish a reconciled relationship with me. In return, I got forgiveness of sins, a feeling of being amazingly clean on the inside, a deep assurance that I will live with God for all eternity, a joy and peace in my heart that is beyond explanation, a sense that God is with me every day helping me make wise decisions and choices, and a feeling of love that goes all the way to the core of my being, even if nobody else on the earth cares. There's really no calculating the rate of return because what fraction of eternity is time, what fraction of infinity is this present reality, what fraction of God's love could my love possibly be?"

If you had been this woman's coworker, how would you have responded?

What is your evaluation of this woman's approach in presenting Christ to a coworker?

How do *you* present Jesus Christ to those you encounter who are not in relationship with Him?

Is there an aspect of your work environment or job description that might allow you to open a conversation about Jesus in a unique way?

S
Supplementary Scriptures to Consider

Peter also said this about our inheritance:

> All of you be of one mind, having compassion for one another; love as brothers, be tenderhearted, be courteous, not returning evil for evil or reviling for reviling, but on the contrary blessing, knowing that you were called to this, that you may inherit a blessing. For
> "He who would love life
> And see good days,
> Let him refrain his tongue from evil,
> And his lips from speaking deceit.
> Let him turn away from evil and do good;
> Let him seek peace and pursue it.
> For the eyes of the LORD are on the righteous,
> And His ears are open to their prayers;
> But the face of the LORD is against those who do evil"
> (1 Pet. 3:8-12).

• Peter believed in an eternal inheritance of everlasting life and a home in heaven that comes to all who accept Jesus as Savior. He also believed in an inheritance of rewards that would be granted according to faithful service. How do you respond to each of these admonitions of Peter that are related to an inheritance of blessing:

Be of one mind:

Have compassion for one another:

Love as brothers:

Be tenderhearted:

Be courteous:

Do not return evil for evil, or reviling for reviling, but on the contrary, blessing:

• To what extent, if any, are these Christlike behaviors contingent on the other person's willingness to participate in the relationship or receive what you give?

• What does it mean to you to "seek peace and pursue it"? (Note: Peace refers to genuine wholeness and reconciliation, not merely the absence of conflict or war.) How do you practically go about seeking reconciliation with those with whom you have disagreements or differences of opinion? How to you actively pursue reconciliation with those who have become estranged from you?

• What do you do if *you* desire reconciliation but the other person rejects reconciliation?

Peter also wrote these words about the incorruptible nature of spiritual rebirth:

> Since you have purified your souls in obeying the truth
> through the Spirit in sincere love of the brethren, love one
> another fervently with a pure heart, having been born again,
> not of corruptible seed but incorruptible, through the word of
> God which lives and abides forever, because
> "All flesh is as grass,
> And all the glory of man as the flower of the grass.
> The grass withers,
> And its flower falls away,
> But the word of the LORD endures forever"
> (1 Pet. 1:22–25).

• Words are generally fleeting and transient. Spoken words, especially, seem to evaporate into the air in which they are uttered. Yet this passage in Peter says something very different about the "word of God" and the "word of the LORD." Note that Jesus was described in the Gospel of John as the Word (John 1:1–4), "In the beginning was the Word, and the Word was with God, and the Word was God. He was in the beginning with God. All things were made through Him, and without Him nothing was made that was made. In Him was life, and the life was the light of men.") What does it mean to you for the Word of God—Jesus Christ—to live and abide *forever*?

- What does it mean for the word that *indwells* you to last forever? What happens to a person who builds their life upon the word of God? What about the word prepares them for eternity? How does the word become inseparably embedded in a person's spirit?

- How do you define the concept "incorruptible seed" in everyday terms?

- According to this passage, what are the prerequisites for a person to live forever and not live as the grass of the field, which is here today and gone tomorrow?

I

Introspection and Implications

1. With what terms do you describe your spiritual inheritance?

2. In what ways is it difficult for a person to believe for a great and glorious eternity when the present is marked by suffering and trouble? Is it easier to believe for a wonderful eternity than to believe for a wonderful tomorrow?

3. Peter quoted a passage from Psalm 34 that says, in effect, "If you want to love your life and experience good days, don't speak evil." Describe in practical terms what this means to you as you follow Jesus day by day.

4. Do you have a sense of deep gratitude for your salvation? How do you express that gratitude to the Lord? To other people?

C
Communicating the Good News

How do you explain the concept of spiritual rebirth to a person who does not know Christ Jesus as their Savior?

Lesson #2

TESTED BY FIERY TRIALS

Fiery Trials: a painful experience intended to determine the performance, quality, and usefulness of a person

B
Bible Focus

> *Beloved, do not think it strange concerning the fiery trial which is to try you, as though some strange thing happened to you; but rejoice to the extent that you partake of Christ's sufferings, that when His glory is revealed, you may also be glad with exceeding joy. If you are reproached for the name of Christ, blessed are you, for the Spirit of glory and of God rests upon you. On their part he is blasphemed, but on your part He is glorified. But let none of you suffer as a murderer, a thief, an evildoer, or as a busybody in other people's matters. Yet if anyone suffers as a Christian, let him not be ashamed, but let him glorify God in this matter. . . .*
>
> *Therefore let those who suffer according to the will of God commit their souls to Him in doing good, as to a faithful Creator (1 Pet. 4:12–16, 19).*

Most of us do all we can to avoid times of trouble or suffering! The truth, however, is that Christians have *always* been persecuted through the ages, to greater and lesser degrees and in a variety of ways. Peter's words were doubly potent in that a number of Christians at the time of his letters were being openly burned alive.

The Jewish Christians perhaps had a better understanding of suffering than the Gentiles since Jews have always been the most persecuted people on the earth. Peter wrote plainly to the early church: persecution is inevitable. It is not a matter of *if* a person will be persecuted, but when, how, and where. It is more likely that a person *will* be persecuted than *not* persecuted. The important issue is *how* a Christian faces persecution.

Persecution continues today. Researchers recently reported that of the nearly two billion Christians alive today, one in ten is experiencing significant persecution for his or her faith. Why? To a great extent, people are resistant to and highly suspicious of change that may upset their social standing, political power, or economic status. Christianity is perceived to be a threat to all three: it challenges the way people get and spend money it confronts those who misuse power, proclaims a higher authority than earthly kings, and it demands that social barriers be removed when it comes to a person's standing before God.

Peter gave this response to persecution: rejoice in it! Peter believed strongly that a particular type of glory rested upon the person who suffered. He likened it to the *Shekinah*, the luminous glow of the presence of God that settled upon Mount Sinai and later filled the tabernacle (Ex. 16:7; 29:43). The persecuted person shares in that glory, but the greater purpose is to reflect glory to God. In other words, if a Christian has to suffer for Christ, he must do so in a way that his suffering brings greater glory—honor and exaltation—to God. A Christian must not think that his suffering for any form of wrongdoing is genuine godly suffering worthy of a God-given reward. To the contrary! Only suffering for the cause of one's belief in Christ Jesus warrants God's reward. Note that among the forms mentioned of non-qualifying wrongdoing are murder, stealing, acting in an evil way toward others, and being a "busybody"! Each of these forms of behavior destroys others and the church to some degree, whether in numbers of members or its appeal to sinners, its integrity, and the morale among believers.

What should Christians do when they face persecution for Christ? Refuse to be ashamed of Christ, give even *greater* witness to the glory and love of God, and make a renewed commitment in their hearts and minds to do good in the name of Christ.

Are you facing persecution today?

Do you believe persecution will increase or decrease for Christians in the days ahead?

How do you respond to your persecutors? What does it mean to you to give God glory in suffering?

A
Application for Today

Pliny, the Roman governor in Asia Minor during the second century, was puzzled by the Christians who were brought before him for trial. He wrote about one of his experiences to Emperor Trajan asking for advice. His letter has become famous in history.

Pliny wrote that a certain unnamed Christian was brought before him, and finding little fault in him, Pliny threatened him by saying, "I will banish you."

"You cannot," came the reply, "for the entire world is my Father's house."

"I will slay you and you will be blotted from eternity," said the Governor.

"You cannot," answered the Christian, "for my life is hid with Christ in God."

"I will take away your possessions," continued Pliny.

"You cannot, for my treasure is in heaven."

"I will drive you away from man and you will have no friend left," was the final threat.

The Christian calmly replied, "You cannot, for I have an unseen Friend from Whom you are not able to separate me."

If you had faced Pliny, what would *you* have said?

These four would-be punishments—banishment, death, loss of possessions, and total loss of friendship—are certainly among the foremost fears many people have when it comes to suffering for their faith. What form might these persecutions take in today's world?

What form of persecution do you fear the most? Have you prepared your heart and mind to confront that type of persecution? How so?

S
Supplementary Scriptures to Consider

Peter also wrote this about suffering trials:

> In this you greatly rejoice, though now for a little while, if need be, you have been grieved by various trials, that the genuineness of your faith, being much more precious than gold that perishes, though it is tested by fire, may be found to praise, honor, and glory at the revelation of Jesus Christ, whom having not seen you love. Though now you do not see Him, yet believing, you rejoice with joy inexpressible and full of glory, receiving the end of your faith—the salvation of your souls (1 Pet. 1:6–9).

• Peter seemed to ask: What is a little suffering in comparison to the inexpressible joy of eternal salvation? How do you respond to such a question?

• Peter saw no comparison between any loss a person might suffer through persecution and the lasting value of genuine faith. Is your faith more valuable than anything you might lose during a time of persecution?

Peter said this to those who were suffering or might suffer:

> And who is he who will harm you if you become followers of what is good? But even if you should suffer for righteousness' sake, you are blessed. "And do not be afraid of their threats, nor be troubled." But sanctify the Lord God in your hearts, and always be ready to give a defense to everyone who asks you a reason for the hope that is in you, with meekness and fear; having a good conscience, that when they defame you as evildoers, those who revile your good conduct in Christ may be ashamed. For it is better, if it is the will of God, to suffer for doing good than for doing evil (1 Pet. 3:13–17).

• In what ways might being a "follower of what is good," displaying "good conduct in Christ," keep a person from being persecuted? Is doing good deeds a certain vaccination against suffering? Why or why not?

- Peter wrote, "If you suffer . . . you are blessed." How do you respond to this statement?

- Peter quoted a passage from Isaiah, which says more fully:

  > "Do not say, 'A conspiracy,'
  > Concerning all that this people call a conspiracy,
  > Nor be afraid of their threats, nor be troubled.
  > The LORD of hosts, Him you shall hallow;
  > Let Him be your fear,
  > And let Him be your dread" (Isaiah 8:12–13).

- How is a fear of the Lord different than a fear of persecutors? How does fear of the Lord eclipse fear of persecution?

- How can people keep from being afraid of or troubled by those who threaten them or their families?

Peter offered an explanation for what happens to the person who undergoes a fiery trial:

> Since Christ suffered for us in the flesh, arm yourselves also with the same mind, for he who has suffered in the flesh has ceased from sin, that he no longer should live the rest of his time in the flesh for the lusts of men, but for the will of God. For we have spent enough of our past lifetime in doing the will of the Gentiles—when we walked in lewdness, lusts, drunkenness, revelries, drinking parties, and abominable idolatries. In regard to these, they think it strange that you do not run with them in the same flood of dissipation, speaking evil of you. They will give an account to Him who is ready to judge the living and the dead (1 Pet. 4:1–5).

• Peter wrote, "He who has suffered in the flesh has ceased from sin." One interpretation of this is that suffering has a certain purifying effect on a person—a person who is confronting physical suffering for the faith has neither inclination nor ability to engage in the behaviors of sin. Another interpretation of this passage says that the suffering Christian who remains true to the faith exhibits to all who see his life that the power of sin is nothing compared to the power of faith. A third interpretation is that the person who has been saved no longer has a desire to sin. How do *you* interpret this passage? Do all three interpretations have a message for your life? If so, what are those messages?

• A man once said, "The guys I used to run with in the neighborhood are now the guys who ridicule me the most." Peter said that those who speak evil of a Christian are very likely those with whom a person formerly associated in a common "flood of dissipation." Can you cite an example of this in your life or among your acquaintances?

Peter gave this admonition for dealing with the devil, the force behind all fiery trials:

> Be sober, be vigilant; because your adversary the devil walks about like a roaring lion, seeking whom he may devour. Resist him, steadfast in the faith, knowing that the same sufferings are experienced by your brotherhood in the world. But may the God of all grace, who called us to His eternal glory by Christ Jesus, after you have suffered a while, perfect, establish, strengthen, and settle you. To Him be the glory and the dominion forever and ever. Amen (1 Pet. 5:8–11).

• How does it make a difference in the way you deal with persecution or a fiery trial to recognize that the source of that persecution is really the devil?

- In what practical ways do you remain sober and vigilant against the adversary of your soul?

- Peter saw the end result of suffering as perfection, establishment, strength, and a settled feeling. Has that been your experience? How so? Do these end results give you hope and courage?

I
Introspection and Implications

1. People who live in Western cultures are well acquainted with the word *compromise*. The word is vital to the functioning of democratic government. To what extent does this word apply to a Christian's expressions of faith in a pluralistic society? Is there ever a situation that warrants compromise of *belief*? A compromise of *behavior* associated with belief?

2. Peter wrote: "Always be ready to give a defense to everyone who asks you a reason for the hope that is in you, with meekness and fear" (1 Pet. 3:15). Do you feel as if you *have* an always-ready defense to offer those who might ask you about your faith? To what extent would you be bold in offering your defense if you knew the person was looking for a justifiable means to persecute you or persecute you further? In what ways is it difficult to give a defense of the faith with *meekness and fear*?

3. Are Christians today being defamed as evildoers? Cite an example. How should a Christian actively confront that defamation?

4. How do you feel about martyrs? What do you fear about the potential for being a martyr?

5. Perhaps the greatest story in the Old Testament about a fiery trial is that of Shadrach, Meshach, and Abed-Nego, who were persecuted for their faith by the Babylonian King Nebuchadezzar. Reread this story in Daniel 3. What about the story stands out to you as a new insight?

C
Communicating the Good News

History shows that, in virtually all cases where martyrdom of Christians occurred on a fairly widespread basis, the kingdom of God flourished in the aftermath. How do you respond to that fact? Why do you believe this occurs?

A woman once said: "I'm not afraid of dying for my faith. I'm just concerned about the suffering before I die. If I have any hesitation in sharing my faith, it's a hesitation related to suffering." Do you agree or disagree with her statement? What fears keep us from engaging in evangelistic activities as frequently, publicly, or as boldly as we might?

LESSON #3

LIVING AND PRECIOUS STONES

Living Stones: human beings united together by Christ's saving grace to be a great fortress of faith, monument of God's love, and sanctuary of forgiveness and comfort

B
Bible Focus

Coming to Him as to a living stone, rejected indeed by men, but chosen by God and precious, you also, as living stones, are being built up a spiritual house, a holy priesthood, to offer up spiritual sacrifices acceptable to God through Jesus Christ.

Therefore it is also contained in the Scripture,

"Behold, I lay in Zion
A chief cornerstone, elect, precious,
And he who believes on Him will by no means be put to shame."

Therefore, to you who believe, He is precious; but to those who are disobedient,

"The stone which the builders rejected
Has become the chief cornerstone,"

and

"A stone of stumbling
And a rock of offense."

They stumble, being disobedient to the word, to which they also were appointed.

But you are a chosen generation, a royal priesthood, a holy nation, His own special people, that you may proclaim the praises of Him who called you out of darkness into His marvelous light; who once were not a people but are now the people of God, who had not obtained mercy but now have obtained mercy (1 Pet. 2:4; 9–10).

Peter reminded the church about the solidity and strength of their faith, using a metaphor with which they were well acquainted. As a building product, *stone* was not only the strongest material in the ancient world, but also the material most likely to last through time. Peter cited three passages from the Old Testament that foretold the Messiah who would be a chosen and precious cornerstone laid in Zion. Even though Jesus was rejected by the religious leaders in Jerusalem, He nonetheless was the chief cornerstone of the Christian faith. Jesus said this of Himself, in fulfillment of the Old Testament passages (Matt. 21:42).

The message was clearly this: you either build on the Rock (Jesus Christ), or you have the judgment of the Rock fall on you.

Peter admonished the early church members to come to Christ "as to a living stone" so that they also, as "living stones," might be built up into a great spiritual house.

The message was this: just as Christ was a living stone, you are living stones. Conduct your lives in such a way that those who are coming after you can build their lives upon your faithful witness—just as stones are laid upon stones to create a great building. And when it comes to those who reject your message, God will use your witness of Christ as a form of judgment upon them.

Peter then reminded the church to recognize their position before God:

- *a chosen generation*—privileged to know Christ and enter into an intimate fellowship with God. Those who read Peter's letter were among the first generation to know what it meant to be saved and fully reconciled with God through Christ Jesus' atoning sacrifice. Although we were not among the first generation to know Christ, we nonetheless are chosen for this same privilege. We must choose to be among the chosen!

- *a royal priesthood*—with full access to God, offering all of our work, worship, and lives to His service.

- *a holy nation*—a body of people who form a spiritual kingdom. Christians hear and obey the words of King Jesus. The word holy, *hagios*, means "different." Christians obey a law and standards that are God's, not the world's.

- *His own special people*—beloved and valued because of who they are in Christ, not for any trait they possess as human beings.

The purpose for being a living stone built into a holy temple—the reason for being part of a chosen generation, a royal priesthood, a holy nation, and a special people—was made clear by Peter. We are to praise God for Christ Jesus and for His mercy extended to us!

Do you have a clear understanding of where you are in history as a "living stone" laid among other living stones to create a great worldwide spiritual house?

Do you have a clear understanding of who *God* says you are as His child and as part of His people?

A
Application for Today

A little boy was scared about his first day at the new school. The family had just moved to the city a few weeks prior to the start of school, and although the boy had made a few friends in his neighborhood, none of them were going to be in his class. His father came to him and said, "I want you to remember all day that your name is Danny and you are a Harrison!"

"Say it aloud," Dad added. "Say, 'MY NAME IS DANNY AND I AM A HARRISON!'"

"My name is Danny and I am a Harrison," the little boy said, but with no real conviction or courage, and certainly not much volume.

"No," said Dad. "Say it like you really know what it means! You were named for the great prophet Daniel, who survived a lion's den and was bold before great kings in ancient times. Not only that, but you are the beloved child of Dottie and Jim Harrison, the grandson of Roger and Martha Harrison, and the great-grandson of Emil and Catherine Harrison. You come from a family that is known for doing good things in this world, a Christian family who are saved and headed for an eternal home in heaven. Your great-grandparents helped establish two churches in their lifetime and they built a great company. Your grandparents expanded that company and founded two schools overseas that teach the Bible to new converts. Your grandparents and great-grandparents on your mother's side of the family were also hard-working, law-abiding, Christian men and women. Your parents are carrying on the traditions of both families. We are here opening a new factory in this city for our family company, and we are involved in a church that is reaching out to needy people in this city and elsewhere. Not only that, but I love you. Your mother loves you. Your grandparents all love you. You are a beloved HARRISON, son! Now say it again."

This time the little boy nearly shouted the words, "MY NAME IS DANNY AND I AM A HARRISON!"

"That's the spirit," said Dad. "Anytime you feel a little fear today, remember who you are and remember who loves you."

If someone asked you today, "Who *are* you?" how would you respond? Beyond your natural family lineage, who are you in Christ Jesus? Why is it important that we occasionally recall—vividly and in detail—who we are in Christ? Why is it important to always keep before us the description that Peter gave to the church: we are a chosen generation, a royal priesthood, a holy nation, a special people?

S
Supplementary Scriptures to Consider

Peter advised the early church members that, even knowing their importance and position in God, they must show respect for those in political authority over them:

Submit yourselves to every ordinance of man for the Lord's sake, whether to the king as supreme, or to governors, as to those who are sent by him for the punishment of evildoers and for the praise of those who do good (1 Pet. 2:13–14).

• To what extent does submission to earthly law bring about the praise of earthly leaders? How does this impact the ability to spread the gospel?

• When a person knows his or her position in Christ Jesus, is it easier or more difficult for that person to tolerate sin in their political leaders? To what extent should a Christian speak out against the evil behavior of a leader who has authority over their lives?

• What does it mean to submit to the law "for the Lord's sake"? (Often when war or civil war grips a nation, public evangelism efforts are nearly always shut down, although a witness for Christ may continue "underground.") In what ways might a rebellion against evil rulers result in a limitation of evangelism?

• Peter noted that one of the reasons for submitting to kings and governors is that they might punish evildoers and, thus, reduce the amount of evil in the greater society as a whole. Can you cite an example of this in your life, city, or nation?

Peter called upon servants to submit to their masters, even as members of a chosen generation, royal priesthood, holy nation, and special people:

> Servants, be submissive to your masters with all fear, not only to the good and gentle, but also the harsh. For this is commendable, if because of conscience toward God one endures grief, suffering wrongfully. For what credit is it if, when you are beaten for your faults, you take it patiently? But when you do good and suffer, if you take it patiently, this is commendable before God (1 Pet. 2:18–20).

• In what ways is it difficult to submit to people who are steeped in sin? (Note: Do not limit this to the greater political arena. Consider those who are in authority over you in the workplace or in a school setting.)

• Peter called upon those who suffer for doing good to suffer *patiently*? How does a person do this in practical ways?

Peter also admonished submission in other areas of life:

1) Wives, likewise, be submissive to your own husbands, that even if some do not obey the word, they, without a word, may be won by the conduct of their wives, when they observe your chaste conduct accompanied by fear. . . .

   Husbands, likewise, dwell with them with understanding, giving honor to the wife, as to the weaker vessel, and as being heirs together of the grace of life, that your prayers may not be hindered" (1 Pet. 3:1–2, 7).

2) Likewise you younger people, submit yourselves to your elders (1 Pet. 5:5).

3) The elders who are among you I exhort . . . Shepherd the flock of God which is among you, serving as overseers, not by compulsion but willingly, not for dishonest gain but eagerly; nor as being lords over those entrusted to you, but being examples to the flock; and when the Chief Shepherd appears, you will receive the crown of glory that does not fade away (1 Pet. 5:1–4).

• How does yielding decision-making power impact the person who is given authority to decide or choose? In what ways does it free the person who yields?

• What is the balance Peter struck between submitting to authority and exercising authority?

• How might submission be likened to the mortar necessary for laying stones on one another in the building process?

I
Introspection and Implications

1. How is it beneficial to remind others around you about their role in Christ Jesus to be a chosen generation, royal priesthood, holy nation, God's own special people? What might be gained by uplifting this role as we train and encourage our children? Our young people in the church?

2. On whose faith, example, or witness has *your* life been laid as a living stone in the building of God's holy temple?

3. Respond to each of these statements made by Paul:

   • You were "called out of darkness into His marvelous light"—
   • You "once were not a people but are now the people of God"—
   • You once "had not obtained mercy but now have obtained mercy"—

4. Peter quoted Isaiah in saying that those who believe on Messiah (Christ Jesus) "will by no means be put to shame." Even so, ascribing shame seems to be a major form of persecution. What does this phrase from Peter mean to you? How do you confront those who try to label you in terms that indicate shame?

C
Communicating the Good News

What do you hold out as the definition of a *Christian* to those you are seeking to win to Christ?

How do you describe the *church* to those who are unsaved?

Lesson #4

PARTAKERS
OF THE DIVINE NATURE

Partakers: to share fully in something

Divine Nature: the character traits of God

B
Bible Focus

> *Grace and peace be multiplied to you in the knowledge of God and of Jesus our Lord, as His divine power has given to us all things that pertain to life and godliness, through the knowledge of Him who called us by glory and virtue, by which have been given to us exceedingly great and precious promises, that through these you may be partakers of the divine nature, having escaped the corruption that is in the world through lust.*
>
> *But also for this very reason, giving all diligence, add to your faith virtue, to virtue knowledge, to knowledge self-control, to self-control perseverance, to perseverance godliness, to godliness brotherly kindness, and to brotherly kindness love. For if these things are yours and abound, you will be neither barren nor unfruitful in the knowledge of our Lord Jesus Christ. For he who lacks these things is short-sighted, even to blindness, and has forgotten that he was cleansed from his old sins.*
>
> *Therefore, brethren, be even more diligent to make your call and election sure, for if you do these things you will never stumble; for so an entrance will be supplied to you abundantly into the everlasting kingdom of our Lord and Savior Jesus Christ (2 Pet. 1:2–11).*

What happens if a new believer in Christ Jesus does not move beyond simple belief in Jesus as *Savior* and begin truly to follow Jesus as *Lord*? He shortchanges himself when it comes to all God's promises for life in general and godliness in particular.

Exceedingly great and precious promises have been *given*, to be sure, but these promises must be actively *received* and *acted upon*.

It is only when we actively seek to develop godly character and behavior that we learn what it means to partake of Christ Jesus and to know Him fully. Knowing *about Christ* is not the same as *knowing Christ*. It is only as one develops an experiential relationship with Christ that a person becomes spiritually mature, bears godly fruit, and earns an abundance of rewards in heaven.

There is a downside, Peter said, in *not* moving forward to follow Jesus as Lord and know Him in His fullness. Such a person may become blind toward Christ, even to the point of "forgetting" he was cleansed from old sins and falling back into old patterns of living.

How does a person build upon a foundation of believing in Jesus as Savior? Peter presented a progressive list of seven steps:

- *add virtue*—do not allow your faith to lie dormant, but take courage and put it to work in your everyday life. The Greek word for virtue in this passage is *arête,* and it literally means operative or efficient excellence. Fertile soil that has not yet been plowed and planted is *arête*. Peter's admonition might be stated, "Begin to plow and plant your faith into the routines and responsibilities of your life!"

- *add knowledge*—the word for knowledge in this passage, *gnosis*, refers to practical applied knowledge that enables a person to make honorable, right decisions and choices. As a Christian begins to live out his faith, he must learn which attitudes, words, and behaviors are most honoring to God.

- *add self-control*—the word for self-control, *egkrateia*, literally means the ability to take a grip on oneself. Fight against unbridled lusts and temptations! Make a choice with your will that you are going to live a godly life!

- *add perseverance*—be steadfast and endure, even if circumstances are stacked against you or you feel weak. Ask the Holy Spirit to strengthen your resolve.

- *add godliness*—the word for godliness, *eusebeia*, has no easy translation, but it means to look in two directions simultaneously—to worship God and give Him what is rightfully His, and to serve fellow mankind and give others what is rightfully theirs. For the Christian, it means loving God with one's whole heart, mind, and strength, as Jesus commanded, and *simultaneously* loving others. This is true godliness, a fulfillment of all the commandments.

- *add brotherly kindness*—choose to show affection to your brothers and sisters in Christ Jesus, even when relationships become troublesome. It is an error to say that you love God if you neglect loving others.

- *add love*—don't limit your love to fellow Christians, but seek to develop genuine love for *all* people—mirroring the way God loves all people—so you might win as many as possible to Christ Jesus.

All must be done diligently, which means with intentional focus and purpose. This "ladder of virtues," as it has been called, is not climbed just once but is intended to be a repeated, ongoing process in every believer's life. Growth in our learning of Christ leads to more growth: the more we live in Him, the more we know Him, and the more we are enabled to display Him to the world.

Are you following Jesus as *Lord*? On what evidence do you base your answer? Which part of the ladder of virtues troubles you the most? Do you know why? What might the Holy Spirit be prompting you to do?

A
Application for Today

"I want to know Jesus better," a young man said to his pastor.

The pastor led him to a storage closet at the back of the church and handed him a rake, a hoe, and several small packets of seeds. "Make a garden here at the back of the church building," the pastor said.

"This will help me know Jesus?" the young man asked.

"Start tomorrow morning," the pastor replied gently. "Make the garden as if you were making it for Jesus to enjoy."

The young man tilled the ground and began to make furrows and plant the seeds. "I don't know what this has to do with knowing You," he said to the Lord, "but I'm believing that You have given me this task to do."

As soon as he left his job each day, the young man went to the church to work on the garden. He divided the ground into sections, gave borders to the sections, and created gravel walkways between the sections. When the time came to plant, he sought advice from other gardeners about which seeds to plant at which times. When pests began to attack the young plants that sprouted from the seeds, he sought advice on how to deal with them. He consulted with others about various techniques for training up some of the plants on stakes and trellises and about when to apply fertilizer and how often to water.

When the weather kept him indoors, he often sat in the doorway of the church with his Bible on his lap, reading God's word and watching his garden through new eyes.

On occasions when friends asked him to leave town for a few days for parties at the beach, he declined their invitations and remained true to his gardening job. At times when his back hurt and he began to question whether the garden was worth the effort, he still showed up to do the work that was there to do.

The young man began to use his time in the garden to talk to God in prayer. Two children began to come regularly to watch him work. Over time, he invited them to help him and they eagerly joined in. As they worked together, he talked to them about God and prayed for them and with them. He shared with them what he was learning about gardening and about being faithful to the Lord.

When the flowering plants began to bloom, he cut bouquets for the church altar and took flowers to church members who were in hospitals or nursing centers. When the vegetable plants began to produce, he prepared baskets of produce and made them available to church members. He took the leftover produce to the food bank that distributed food to the poor.

As winter approached, the pastor went to the young man and said, "Do you know Jesus better than you did this time last year?"

The young man smiled broadly, "Oh yes, He's the Senior Gardener of this garden!"

"And you, my young friend," the pastor said, "have become His apprentice and friend."

How did this young man's experience manifest the ladder of virtues?

How is the Lord leading you to *apply* your faith to the work He has placed before you?

S
Supplementary Scriptures to Consider

Peter also said this about godly behavior:

> Abstain from fleshly lusts which war against the soul, having your conduct honorable among the Gentiles, that when they speak against you as evildoers, they may, by your good works which they observe, glorify God in the day of visitation (1 Pet. 2:11–12).

• *Fleshly lusts* referred to more than the physical nature of a human being. It referred to *human nature* and to a life without the standards and help of Christ. The phrase referred to everything that was contrary to godly living. In what ways do you find it difficult to abstain from *all* things that are contrary to godly living?

• The "day of visitation" was a term used to describe the return of Christ. This day was believed to be marked primarily by judgment. Peter said that the good works of the Christians would glorify God in that day— even if nobody in the here-and-now recognized a person's good works for what they were, God ultimately would honor those works. How do you deal with delayed recognition for the good deeds you do in the name of Christ? Do you have difficulty with Peter's words that your good deeds will one day cause unbelievers to glorify *God*—and not glorify *you*?

In addition to developing personal character, Peter said this about rewards from God:

> All of you be submissive to one another, and be clothed with humility, for
> "God resists the proud,
> But gives grace to the humble."
> Therefore humble yourselves under the mighty hand of God,
> that He may exalt you in due time, casting all your care upon
> Him, for He cares for you (1 Pet. 5:5–7).

• What does it mean for believers to be "submissive to one another"? How is this related to godliness and brotherly kindness?

• Peter linked humility with God's exalting us in due time. When do you believe that time will occur? What does it mean to be exalted?

• How difficult is it to cast *all* of our cares upon God? How do we do this?

Peter told the church to be *diligent* in adding virtues and other godly attributes to their faith. He also said this:

> Be diligent to be found by Him in peace, without spot and blameless; and consider that the longsuffering of our Lord is salvation (2 Pet. 3:14–15).

• What does it mean to be "diligent to be found by Him in peace"? This was written to the church as a whole. What does it mean to you? To what extent do you believe the church is "in peace" today?

• Can a Christian be truly blameless and without spot? Or is this a goal that is worth pursuing but cannot be fully reached in this life? On what evidence do you base your answer?

- Peter contended that the longsuffering patience of the Lord gives greater opportunity for souls to be saved. As much as we might long for Christ to return, to what extent are we wise to pray that the Lord delays His return?

Peter wrote this about our efforts to turn away from former fleshly lusts and seek, instead, to live in a holy manner:

> Gird up the loins of your mind, be sober, and rest your hope fully upon the grace that is to be brought to you at the revelation of Jesus Christ; as obedient children, not conforming yourselves to the former lusts, as in your ignorance; but as He who called you is holy, you also be holy in all your conduct, because it is written, "Be holy, for I am holy" (1 Pet. 1:13–16).

- How does a person "gird" the mind?

- Do we make ourselves holy, or does God make us holy? What is our part?

I

Introspection and Implications

1. Peter wrote that Christians become "partakers of the divine nature" (2 Pet. 1:4). What does this mean to you?

2. In your faith walk with the Lord, have you seen the ladder of virtues at work since you accepted Jesus as your Savior? How so?

3. The longer you follow Jesus as Lord, do you find that you are more certain about your standing in Christ and your relationship with God? How does this certainty impact your attitudes, speech, and daily behavior?

4. In what ways is it difficult to be consistently *diligent* in one's faith walk with the Lord? How does the Holy Spirit help you remain diligent?

C
Communicating the Good News

"I don't think I can ever be a really good Christian. I just don't think I will ever be able to change some of my old sinful habits." How would you respond to a person who made such a statement? Would your response vary according to whether the person was an unbeliever or a believer in Christ?

LESSON #5

REMAINING STEADFAST IN THE LIGHT

Steadfast: unwavering, firmly fixed, and constant in purpose, loyalty, and resolve

B
Bible Focus

> We did not follow cunningly devised fables when we made
> known to you the power and coming of our Lord Jesus Christ,
> but were eyewitnesses of His majesty. For He received from
> God the Father honor and glory when such a voice came to
> Him from the Excellent Glory: "This is My beloved Son, in
> whom I am well pleased." And we heard this voice which
> came from heaven when we were with Him on the holy moun-
> tain.
>
> And so we have the prophetic word confirmed, which you
> do well to heed as a light that shines in a dark place, until the
> day dawns and the morning star rises in your hearts; knowing
> this first, that no prophecy of Scripture is of any private
> interpretation, for prophecy never came by the will of man, but
> holy men of God spoke as they were moved by the Holy Spirit
> (2 Pet. 1:16–21).

False teachers rather quickly invaded the early church, some of them
advocating a need for keeping all the Jewish law, others mixing Christian
doctrine with Greek philosophy, and some questioning the reliability of the
messages conveyed by the apostles. Certainly many of the events surrounding the life, ministry, death, and resurrection of Jesus were so miraculous to
both Jews and Gentiles that they must have seemed almost unbelievable.
This is understandable, especially if we consider that these early believers
did not have the full New Testament as we have it today. Many of them had
heard about the incidents in Jesus' life from second-hand or third-hand
preachers and teachers. Peter wrote to say, as an apostle, "I was among the
eyewitnesses of His majesty!"

Peter referred to perhaps the most stunning event of his experience with
Jesus during Jesus' personal ministry: the transfiguration of Jesus, during
which Peter, James, and John saw Jesus become radiant in appearance while
consulting with Moses and Elijah. They heard the voice of God proclaiming,
"This is My beloved Son, in whom I am well pleased. Hear Him!"
(Matt. 17:5).

The accusations continue today that the accounts of Jesus' life were
"cunningly devised fables." To those, however, who have first-hand knowledge of the *reality* of Christ Jesus in their lives—their own experiences with
the saving power of Jesus no less miraculous than those of the first believers—the gospel message is *real truth*.

Peter specifically used the word *prophecy*, which is not limited to the
foretelling of the future but is primarily the *forthtelling* of God's Word.

Prophecy is the proclamation of the truth of God and the expression of God's will in response to any human circumstance or behavior.

Peter made three statements about prophecy that we are wise to heed.

First, Jesus confirmed what all of the Old Testament prophets said about Messiah. Peter and the other apostles in the first century believed that the Holy Spirit had "moved" the writers of Scripture to record the words we have in the Bible. The word we usually translate as *moved* is *phero*, which literally means to "carry along" or "sweep upward." The Holy Spirit was perceived to have uplifted the minds of those chosen to write the Scriptures, giving these prophets a glimpse into the very heart and mind of God. They were privileged to see into eternity, and then attempt to encapsulate eternal truth into the finite language of earthly time. It was God who *initiated* the prophetic word, nearly always without any desire on the part of the prophet to be a chosen vessel for pouring out God's word.

Peter wrote to declare, "We know the prophecies about Christ Jesus are true because we have seen them fulfilled—we were lifted to spiritual heights in following Jesus. We saw into eternity, just as the prophets of old, and the Holy Spirit confirmed to us that Jesus is the Son of God." We can trust the Holy Spirit today to raise our awareness to new heights to understand the ways in which Jesus fulfilled all of God's great plan for reconciliation between man and God. On our own, we cannot fully understand the infinite love and mercy of God, but we can trust that His love and mercy were embodied in Christ Jesus, God made flesh.

Second, even if we do not understand fully with our rational minds all the hows and whys associated with what Jesus said and did, we can still believe what the Scriptures say about Him. Peter admonished the church to heed the prophecies "as a light that shines in a dark place, until the day dawns and the morning star rises in your hearts" (v. 19). We do not need to *know* in order to *believe.*

Third, no prophecy is subject to private interpretation. In the Old Testament one of the marks of a false prophet was that he spoke his own words rather than the words of God. The prophet Jeremiah said of false prophets, "They speak a vision of their own heart, not from the mouth of the LORD" (Jeremiah 23:16). Every "word" that we hear from the Lord, we must verify against Scripture and against early church writings and the beliefs common to the church around the world and through all ages. We are wise to verify what we believe as we consult those who have devoted their lives to a careful study of the Scriptures. If what we have concluded varies, we should examine humbly whether we are speaking from our own wishes and desires. True prophecy, Peter said, "never came by the will of man."

Peter not only gave us greater understanding about how we each should approach Scripture and about the prophecies related to Christ Jesus, but also gave us insight into how we might evaluate the "words" others give us as prophecies from the Lord:

- Check what is said against Scripture.

- Check the motivation of the speaker and the way in which the speaker came to his or her message.

- Check what other godly people have said or are saying on the same subject.

False teachers are no less common to our churches today than they were to the churches Peter addressed.

Have you ever experienced or heard a prophecy that you found troubling? What did you do? What was the outcome?

A
Application for Today

"How do you *know* that?" a six-year-old girl asked her older friend, who had just rattled off the multiplication tables from one times one to nine times eight.

"I learned it in school," the older girl said matter-of-factly.

"But how do you *know* that nine times eight is seventy-two?" asked the younger girl.

The older girl couldn't come up with a quick answer other than to say, "I just *know*. When you get to third grade, you'll know, too!"

The younger girl went home and asked her father, "Do you believe nine times eight is seventy-two?"

"What a question!" her father said lightheartedly and in surprise. "Who told you about the times tables?"

The little girl replied, "Angie said that nine times eight is seventy-two. What do you say?"

Her father took a blank piece of paper and pen and sat down with his daughter. He drew dots on the paper and showed his daughter how a grid of dots that was nine dots across and eight dots down produced seventy-two dots.

"So," the little girl said after sitting through her father's fairly lengthy explanation and counting all the dots on the page, "you believe nine times eight is seventy-two?"

"Yes," said her father.

"Well," the little girl said, "why didn't you just say so."

The little girl hadn't wanted to *learn* the multiplication tables or the mathematical rationale for them; she had just wanted to know what her father *believed*. If *he* said nine times eight was seventy-two, it surely must be!

In what areas of our faith walk with Christ Jesus is it enough simply to believe without questioning? In what areas should we question in order to learn more about Christ? In what ways should all of our learning be geared toward a greater depth of ability to *believe*?

S
Supplementary Scriptures to Consider

Peter said this about Christ:

> And if you call on the Father, who without partiality judges according to each one's work, conduct yourselves throughout the time of your stay here in fear; knowing that you were not redeemed with corruptible things, like silver or gold, from your aimless conduct received by tradition from your fathers, but with the precious blood of Christ, as of a lamb without blemish and without spot. He indeed was foreordained before the foundation of the world, but was manifest in these last times for you who through Him believe in God, who raised Him from the dead and gave Him glory, so that your faith and hope are in God (1 Pet. 1:17–21).

• Peter made it very clear that a person cannot buy his way into salvation or redeem himself through any corruptible things or works. He likened this to "aimless conduct" that a person develops as a result of adopting human traditions, whether cultural or religious. Have you ever encountered teachings regarding things a person must do in order to earn salvation? How did you respond?

- Note the phrase "foreordained before the foundation of the world." What does this mean to you? In what ways did the prophets of old reveal that Christ was foreordained?

- Peter wrote that God our Father "without partiality judges according to each one's work." If we cannot work our way into salvation, what is it that God the Father is judging, and to what end?

- How was Jesus manifested to you so that you made the decision to believe in Him and put your faith and hope in God?

Peter said this about the word of God:

> Laying aside all malice, all deceit, hypocrisy, envy, and all evil speaking, as newborn babes, desire the pure milk of the word, that you may grow thereby, if indeed you have tasted that the Lord is gracious (1 Pet. 2:1–3).

- As noted earlier, prophecy is primarily the *forthtelling* of God's Word. How does the word of God produce spiritual growth? What has been your experience? What have you gained from careful reading and study of God's Word?

- Why did Peter say it is important to lay aside all malice, deceit, hypocrisy, envy, and evil speaking? Can a person ever fully receive the spiritual nourishment of God's Word if he or she approaches God's Word with an attitude of malice? If he thinks the Word is filled with deceit? If he believes that receiving God's Word leads to hypocrisy, envy, or speaking evil?

- Newborn babies are hungry—voraciously so, and often! Do you approach God's Word as a newborn babe?

Peter recognized that Paul had also written a prophetic word to the churches Peter was addressing:

> As also our beloved brother Paul, according to the wisdom
> given to him, has written to you, as also in all his epistles,
> speaking in them of these things, in which are some things
> hard to understand, which untaught and unstable people twist
> to their own destruction, as they do also the rest of the Scrip-
> tures. You therefore, beloved, since you know this beforehand,
> beware lest you also fall from your own steadfastness, being
> led away with the error of the wicked; but grow in the grace
> and knowledge of our Lord and Savior Jesus Christ
> (2 Pet. 3:15–18).

- Is it inevitable that, when people find something hard to understand, they twist it to conform to their own interpretation? How do we avoid this in ourselves? How do we evaluate whether this is happening as we hear others teach or interpret the Scriptures?

- How does a person avoid "being led away with the error of the wicked"? What practical steps do you take to keep yourself from being swayed by false teaching or false interpretation?

• What does it mean to you to grow in the *grace* of our Lord and Savior Jesus Christ?

• What does it mean to you to grow in *knowledge* of our Lord and Savior Jesus Christ?

Peter encouraged believers that it *is* possible to know the truth and follow it:

> If God did not spare the angels who sinned, but cast them down to hell and delivered them into chains of darkness, to be reserved for judgment; and did not spare the ancient world, but saved Noah, one of eight people, a preacher of righteousness, bringing in the flood on the world of the ungodly; and turning the cities of Sodom and Gomorrah into ashes, condemned them to destruction, making them an example to those who afterward would live ungodly; and delivered righteous Lot, who was oppressed by the filthy conduct of the wicked (for that righteous man, dwelling among them, tormented his righteous soul from day to day by seeing and hearing their lawless deeds)—then the Lord knows how to deliver the godly out of temptations and to reserve the unjust under punishment for the day of judgment, and especially those who walk according to the flesh in the lust of uncleanness and despise authority (2 Pet. 2:4–10).

- One of the greatest temptations a believer faces is the temptation to question and doubt what the Bible says about Jesus, instead turning away to false teachings that seem plausible, realistic, or comfortable. Respond to Peter's statement that "the Lord knows how to deliver the godly out of temptations." How have you experienced this in your life?

- What is the role we have as followers? How do we wisely follow those in spiritual authority over us? What are we to do if a leader succumbs to behavior that reflects uncleanness? How do we question authority without despising it?

- Peter cited two Old Testament examples in which only a *few* people heeded the truth and were spared horrific consequences. How can we ensure that we will avoid God's judgment for believing a lie? What can a person do today to ensure that he is responding fully to the *truth*?

I
Introspection and Implications

1. When you hear words described as prophetic, do you respond with eagerness or reluctance? Are you open to prophetic words? Are you suspicious of them?

2. Do you regularly approach God's Word as if it is a prophetic (forthtelling) word to you of God's truth for *your* life? If not, why not? If so, what have you experienced?

3. What has God spoken to your heart and mind about who Jesus is? Who you are? How He desires to relate to you? How He desires for you to relate to others? How have you confirmed that this truly was God's message to you and not simply your own desire?

C
Communicating the Good News

In what ways is sharing a person's personal testimony the uttering of a prophetic (forthtelling) word?

In what ways is it better to couch our personal testimony in terms of "I believe" rather than "I know"? Is sharing what we *believe* in any way less powerful than sharing what we know? If so, how so? If not, why not?

Lesson #6

REJECTING FALSE TEACHING

Heresy: adherence to an opinion or belief that contradicts established biblical teaching or biblical authority

B
Bible Focus

> There were also false prophets among the people, even as
> there will be false teachers among you, who will secretly bring
> in destructive heresies, even denying the Lord who bought
> them, and bring on themselves swift destruction. And many
> will follow their destructive ways, because of whom the way of
> truth will be blasphemed. By covetousness they will exploit
> you with deceptive words; for a long time their judgment has
> not been idle, and their destruction does not slumber . . .
>
> These, like natural brutal beasts made to be caught and
> destroyed, speak evil of the things they do not understand, and
> will utterly perish in their own corruption, and will receive the
> wages of unrighteousness, as those who count it pleasure to
> carouse in the daytime. They are spots and blemishes, carous-
> ing in their own deceptions while they feast with you, having
> eyes full of adultery and that cannot cease from sin, enticing
> unstable souls. They have a heart trained in covetous prac-
> tices, and are accursed children. They have forsaken the right
> way and gone astray, following the way of Balaam the son of
> Beor, who loved the wages of unrighteousness; but he was
> rebuked for his iniquity: a dumb donkey speaking with a man's
> voice restrained the madness of the prophet
> (2 Pet. 2:1–3, 12–16).

After encouraging the church to be quick to confirm the prophetic word
about Christ Jesus, Peter took on those who were false prophets infecting the
church. His words were among the most scathing written by New Testament
leaders.

Peter described the false prophets as being motivated by covetousness
regarding financial gain as the primary reason they presented a deception to
the people. Who were they enticing with their inaccurate messages and
heresies? Peter described their victims as "unstable souls." The eventual fate
of these false prophets? Peter stated in very vivid terms that they would one
day "utterly perish in their own corruption."

At issue were "destructive heresies." The word heresy was initially an
honorable word. It was derived from the Greek verb *haireisthai*, which
means "to choose." Thus, a heresy referred to a line of belief or action a
person had chosen for himself. Christianity changed the meaning of the
word!

Before the coming of Jesus Christ, there was no embodiment of definitive, God-given truth. Jesus, however, stated boldly and clearly, "I am the truth" (John 14:6). Prior to Christ, a Gentile might have been presented a number of belief alternatives, any one of which he was free to choose. Even a Jew had a number of belief alternatives regarding interpretations of how best to keep the law, depending upon which line of rabbinic teaching he chose to follow. After Christ, a Gentile seeking to become a Christian either had to accept or reject the truth of Christ Jesus. Thus, a heretic in the church became a person who believed what he *wanted* to believe rather than accept the truth of God.

The false prophets to whom Peter referred were self-styled teachers who were attempting to persuade people to believe things they *wished* were true, rather than what God had said was true. They subtly set themselves up to be fine Christians, and under the guise of self-defined piety, they attempted to convince the believers in the early church to exercise their right to choose what worked for them. They saw this as the ultimate form of freedom in Christ—to map out one's own doctrines and create a new law suited to each individual or group. The message was certainly an enticing one to those who were not well grounded in their faith. According to the teachings of the false prophets, a person could have what he wanted and what God wanted simultaneously. "No!" said Peter sternly. "The Christian who does not accept the truth of Christ Jesus in its entirety without changing it is a person who is really rejecting the truth."

In the end those who teach heresy lead people further away from Christ instead of leading them toward Christ. They teach others to sin while professing to love the Lord. Their work was insidious in the first century, and it is insidious today.

Do you hear heretical statements voiced by people who call themselves Christians?

Has heresy infected your church or denomination?

A
Application for Today

"I don't think Jesus really *meant* that," one man said, "if He even said it. He didn't put down people of other religions."

"I know that *my* God would never send anybody to hell. My God is loving," a second man said with confidence.

"You sound so intolerant," a third person chimed in. "God accepts everybody just as they are."

"That's right!" a fourth person said. "Jesus died for the sins of everybody. Nobody is going to hell. Everybody has already been saved by Jesus."

"You are acting as if there is absolute truth. There's no truth that is universal and absolute for everybody. Each person finds his own truth," yet another person added. "Every religion leads a person to God if a person practices that religion faithfully."

"And there is no sin, either," said a sixth person. "Sin is just a metaphor for deep misunderstandings and disagreements that lead to bad behavior. We need to love one another more and seek to understand one another more. That will put an end to sin. Love is the highest form of tolerance for other people and their opinions. If there is an absolute sin, it's intolerance!"

What gave rise to this onslaught of adamantly stated opinions?

A person had said simply, "I take Jesus at His word and Jesus said, 'I am the way, the truth, and the life. No one comes to the Father except through Me" (John 14:6).

What would *you* have said if you had been in the room where the above statements were voiced?

S
Supplementary Scriptures to Consider

Peter saw the teachings of the false prophets as full of empty words and promises:

> These are wells without water, clouds carried by a tempest,
> for whom is reserved the blackness of darkness forever"
> (2 Pet. 2:17).

- Peter regarded the false teachers as rain clouds that appeared to promise relief from a drought but were carried away by gusts of winds, and in the end, gave nothing that satisfied the soul. How does a person avoid being influenced by people who sound good but really say nothing? How do we detect messages that sound good but in truth are not good?

• Describe the disappointment a person feels when he thinks he is going to receive life-saving or life-enriching information and discovers that nothing about the message is either applicable or meaningful to his life. Have you ever felt this way about someone who tried to sell you something, convince you of something, or promised insider information about something? How did you respond?

Peter described the allure of the false prophets:

> For when they speak great swelling words of emptiness, they allure through the lusts of the flesh, through lewdness, the ones who have actually escaped from those who live in error. While they promise them liberty, they themselves are slaves of corruption; for by whom a person is overcome, by him also he is brought into bondage (2 Pet. 2:18–19).

• The *lusts of the flesh* are all human desires that seek immediate gratification, regardless of the means or cost. False teachers were telling the church that because Jesus died to set men free of the bondage of sin, believers ultimately were free to express themselves and free to participate in any activity they found pleasurable. Why is this *not* true?

- How might a person who offers a false understanding of freedom put others into greater bondage? (Consider the influence of many cult leaders who offer their followers a freedom from the tyranny of social norms and cultural biases.)

Peter argued that a person who turns to Christ because he seeks to escape the polluting sin of the world is actually in danger of being in even greater bondage to sin if he follows the teachings of a false prophet:

> For if, after they have escaped the pollutions of the world
> through the knowledge of the Lord and Savior Jesus Christ,
> they are again entangled in them and overcome, the latter end
> is worse for them than the beginning. For it would have been
> better for them not to have known the way of righteousness,
> than having known it, to turn from the holy commandment
> delivered to them. But it has happened to them according
> to the true proverb: "A dog returns to his own vomit," and,
> "a sow, having washed, to her wallowing in the mire"
> (2 Pet. 2:20–22).

- One of the foremost appeals of the false prophets was this: a believer could believe what he chose to believe for his own self-fulfillment. How might a person be truly set free from his own desires for self-expression and self-determination?

Can a person ever truly fulfill himself—totally satisfy himself and give meaning to his own life?

Peter sharply criticized the attitude and the outspoken behavior of the false prophets:

> They are presumptuous, self-willed. They are not afraid to speak evil of dignitaries, whereas angels, who are greater in power and might, do not bring a reviling accusation against them before the Lord (2 Pet. 2:10–11).

• Define *presumptuous* in your own words. (One dictionary definition says, "inconsiderate, disrespectful, or overconfident—doing something when not entitled or qualified to do it.")

• What is the error of being self-willed? How does this differ from being strong-willed? How does it differ from being submissive, a major theme in Peter's writings?

• Are you afraid to speak evil of dignitaries (those in authority)? Why or why not?

I
Introspection and Implications

1. *In his first letter, Peter stated that Jesus was the sacrificial lamb without spot or blemish* (1 Pet. 1:19). Under the religious laws of Judaism, a lamb was considered unacceptable for sacrifice if it had flaws of any kind. In denouncing the false prophets, Peter stated that they were "spots and blemishes" on the church (2 Pet. 2:13). Again, the meaning is that they were unacceptable blights—their existence in the church made the church flawed and unworthy in God's eyes. How do you define a spot or blemish? How can a person avoid becoming one in the Body of Christ? How should we encourage one another to remain without spot or blemish?

2. *Peter described the false prophets in a number of ways.* Describe what you believe Peter meant in saying the false teachers were:

- "natural brute beasts made to be caught and destroyed" (2 Pet. 2:12)—

- people with hearts "trained in covetous practices" (2 Pet. 2:14)—

- "accursed children" (2 Pet. 2:14)—

- "wells without water" (2 Pet. 2:17)—

3. *Learn to spot a false teacher.* Have you ever encountered a false prophet or a false teacher? How did you know the person was false? What did you do? What was the outcome?

C
Communicating the Good News

To what extent is it imperative that the gospel be presented as absolute truth?

In sharing the good news that Jesus came to be the "way, the truth, and the life" how do you define each of these terms:

• Way:

• Truth:

• Life:

LESSON #7

LOOKING FOR CHRIST'S COMING

Slack: not showing enough care, attention, or energetic rigor

B
Bible Focus

> Beloved, I now write to you this second epistle (in both of
> which I stir up your pure minds by way of reminder), that you
> may be mindful of the words which were spoken before by the
> holy prophets, and of the commandment of us, the apostles of
> the Lord and Savior, knowing this first: that scoffers will come
> in the last days, walking according to their own lusts, and
> saying, "Where is the promise of His coming? For since the
> fathers fell asleep, all things continue as they were from the
> beginning of creation." For this they willfully forget: that by
> the word of God the heavens were of old, and the earth
> standing out of water and in the water, by which the world
> that then existed perished, being flooded with water. But the
> heavens and the earth which are now preserved by the same
> word, are reserved for fire until the day of judgment and
> perdition of ungodly men.
>
> But, beloved, do not forget this one thing, that with the Lord
> one day is as a thousand years, and a thousand years as one
> day. The Lord is not slack concerning His promise, as some
> count slackness, but is longsuffering toward us, not willing
> that any should perish but that all should come to repentance
> (2 Pet. 3:1–9).

Earlier in his letter, Peter had called upon the church to remember that the
prophecies of old were fulfilled in Christ Jesus. He recognized that some
might question how Jesus had fulfilled the prophecies related to His rule and
reign over the earth, or more specifically, his Second Coming.

Peter addressed this concern by saying four things:

First, the prophets foretold that scoffers would come, raising those very
questions about Christ's sovereignty, and their existence would be a sign of
the last days.

Second, Peter reminded them that an end *is* coming. Just when people are
convinced that nothing would ever change, great change can occur! Earlier
in his letter, Peter had mentioned life in the days of Noah and life in the
cities of Sodom and Gomorrah. Surely the people in Noah's day did not
believe their world was about to end—until the rain began and didn't stop.
Surely the people in Sodom and Gomorrah awoke expecting nothing in their
world to change—by nightfall of that same day, they and their cities were in
ashes. The end may not be *expected*, but an end is coming nonetheless.

Third, Peter made it clear that God does not regard time as human beings do. God sees things as states of being, not ticks on a clock. He acts from the infinite glories of eternity, not according to a human understanding of chronology or deadlines.

Fourth, Peter stated that the fact that Jesus hasn't already returned is neither a sign of weakness or impotence on God's part nor a sign that God did not mean what He said—rather it is a sign of God's patience, allowing more and more people to hear the gospel, respond to it, and be cleansed of their sins and granted the gift of eternal life. God's *desire* for mankind is that all mankind will desire Him. Even though this is not presently the case, and may never be, God's desire is still that *all* come to repentance, confess their sins, receive forgiveness, and amend their lives to obey Him. Rather than be concerned with the fact that Jesus has not come back today, we should ask ourselves, "What have I done today to win someone to Christ so that person will be ready for Christ's return?"

Are you impatient for the Lord to return?

Are you happy or sad that the Lord did not return yesterday?

How does believing in the Lord's return impact the way you live from day to day?

How difficult is it to be ready at *all* times for the Lord's return?

A
Application for Today

Grandma found her young grandson sitting on the front porch with silent tears streaming down his face. "What's wrong?" she asked gently, pulling him close to her.

"I don't want Jesus to come today," the little boy said. The family had just finished Sunday lunch and much of the conversation had been about their pastor's sermon on the second coming of Christ. Various family members had eagerly and joyously shared how much better they thought the world would be after Jesus returned to establish His kingdom.

"Why don't you want Jesus to come today?" Grandma asked softly.

"Because Daddy said he's taking me to the city to see a baseball game next Saturday!" the boy said. "I don't want to miss it!"

Is there something you don't want to miss doing or experiencing in your life should Christ Jesus return today? Are there goals you still want to meet and good works you still want to accomplish?

What would be *good* about Christ's return today?

What might be the downside? For example, is there someone you love who isn't ready to meet the Lord? Are you still hoping and believing that person will make a decision for Christ? Do you need to reconcile with or forgive someone before Christ returns?

Do you believe Jesus Christ *will* return in your lifetime? What if He doesn't? Will you feel shortchanged in any way?

S
Supplementary Scriptures to Consider

Peter wrote this about the day of the Lord:

> But the day of the Lord will come as a thief in the night, in which the heavens will pass away with a great noise, and the elements will melt with fervent heat; both the earth and the works that are in it will be burned up. Therefore, since all these things will be dissolved, what manner of persons ought you to be in holy conduct and godliness, looking for and hastening the coming of the day of God, because of which the heavens will be dissolved, being on fire, and the elements will melt with fervent heat? Nevertheless we, according to His promise, look for new heavens and a new earth in which righteousness dwells (2 Pet. 3:10–14).

• Are you really *ready* for the world as you know it to end? Are you *ready* for the earth to be renovated by fire and for all human works and unrighteous people to be destroyed?

- If a person truly believes that all human accomplishments will be burned up in the judgment of God, how might that person's perspective change regarding work? Regarding acquisition of wealth or possessions? Regarding ministry priorities?

- What are your personal hopes for "new heavens and a new earth"? Describe the new cosmos in which you believe you will one day dwell.

Peter explicitly instructs us how to await the coming of Christ:

> The end of all things is at hand; therefore be serious and watchful in your prayers. And above all things have fervent love for one another for "love will cover a multitude of sins." Be hospitable to one another without grumbling. As each one has received a gift, minister it to one another, as good stewards of the manifold grace of God. If anyone speaks, let him speak as the oracles of God. If anyone ministers, let him do it as with the ability which God supplies, that in all things God may be glorified through Jesus Christ, to whom belong the glory and the dominion forever and ever. Amen. (1 Pet. 4:7–11).

• What does it mean to be "serious and watchful" in one's prayers?

• How does fervent love for one another cover sins?

• What are the challenges of being hospitable without grumbling?

• How does using your gifts in ministry to other people qualify you as a "good steward of the manifold grace of God"?

- What does it mean to speak as an "oracle of God"? (An oracle was a person considered to be a source of knowledge or wisdom, giving advice generally in times of trouble or uncertainty.)

- In what practical ways do you look to God to supply the ability you need to be an effective minister of your gifts?

I
Introspection and Implications

1. Peter wrote, "The Lord is not slack concerning His promise, as some count slackness, but is longsuffering toward us" (2 Pet. 3:9). Have you ever felt that the Lord was slack concerning a promise you believed He had made to you? Why did you hold that belief? In what ways might the Lord have been longsuffering toward you, perhaps giving you time to grow spiritually, repent of hindering sins, develop a new understanding of His promise, or develop new abilities required for you to handle the fulfillment of His promise wisely?

2. What challenges do we face in trying to comprehend eternity?

3. Are there specific ways in which you believe God is challenging you to become better prepared for His return? What are you being directed by the Holy Spirit to change in your life?

C
Communicating the Good News

How does the Second Coming impact our urgency to reach others for Christ?

To what degree should news of the Second Coming be part of our evangelistic messages?

NOTES TO LEADERS
OF SMALL GROUPS

As the leader of a small discussion group, think of yourself as a facilitator with three main roles:

- Get the discussion started.

- Involve every person in the group.

- Encourage an open, candid discussion that remains Bible-focused.

You certainly don't need to be the person with all the answers! In truth, much of your role is to be a person who asks questions:

- What really impacted you most in this lesson?

- Was there a particular part of the lesson or a question that you found troubling?

- Was there a particular part of the lesson that you found encouraging or insightful?

- Was there a particular part of the lesson that you'd like to explore further?

Express to the group at the outset of your study that your goal as a group is to gain new insights into God's Word; this is not the forum for defending a point of doctrine or a theological opinion. Stay focused on what God's Word says and means. The purpose of the study is also to share insights on how to apply God's Word to everyday life. *Every* person in the group can and should contribute. The collective wisdom that flows from Bible-focused discussion is often very rich and deep.

Seek to create an environment in which every member of the group feels free to ask questions of other members in order to gain greater understanding. Encourage the group members to voice their appreciation to one another for new insights gained and be supportive of one another. Take the lead in this. Genuinely appreciate and value the contributions made by each person.

Since the letters of Paul are geared to our personal Christian lives as well as to the life of the church as a whole, you may experience a tendency in your group sessions to become overly critical of your *own* church or church leaders. Avoid the tendency to create discord or dissatisfaction. Don't use this Bible study as an opportunity to spread rumor, air anyone's dirty laundry, or criticize your pastor. Rather, seek positive ways to build up one another, including your church leaders. Seek positive outcomes and solutions to any problems you may identify.

You may want to begin each study by having one or more members of the group read through the section provided under "Bible Focus." Ask the group specifically if it desires to discuss any of the questions under the "Application" section, the "Supplemental Scriptures" section, and the "Implications" and "Communicating the Gospel" sections. You do not need to bring closure—or come to a definitive conclusion or consensus—about any one question asked in this study. Rather, if the group does not *have* a satisfactory Bible-based answer, encourage them to engage in further "asking, seeking, and knocking" strategies to discover the answers! Remember the words of Jesus: "Ask, and it will be given to you, seek, and you will find; knock, and it will be opened to you. For everyone who asks receives, and he who seeks finds, and to him who knocks it will be opened" (Matthew 7:7–8).

Finally, open and close your study with prayer. Ask the Holy Spirit, whom Jesus called the Spirit of Truth, to guide your discussion and to reveal what is of eternal benefit to you individually and as a group. As you close your study, ask the Holy Spirit to seal to your remembrance what you have read and studied and to show you in the upcoming days, weeks, and months *ways* to apply what you have studied to your daily life and relationships.

General Themes for the Lessons

Each lesson in this study has one or more core themes. Continually pull the group back to these themes. You can do this by asking simple questions, such as, "How does that relate to _____?" or "How does that help us better understand the concept of _____?" or "In what ways does that help us apply the principle of _____?"

A summary of general themes or concepts in each lesson is provided below:

Lesson #1
RECIPIENTS OF A HEAVENLY INHERITANCE
Spiritual rebirth

The inheritance of the believer—now, and in eternity

Lesson #2
TESTED BY FIERY TRIALS
Preparing for persecution

Godly behavior during times of persecution

Purposes for suffering

Lesson #3
LIVING AND PRECIOUS STONES
What it means to be a "living stone"

What it means to be part of a "chosen generation"

What it means to be part of a "royal priesthood"

What it means to be part of a "holy nation"

What it means to be one of God's own "special people"

The role of submission as we are being built into a "spiritual house"

Lesson #4
PARTAKERS OF THE DIVINE NATURE
Following Jesus not only as Savior, but as Lord

The ladder of virtues

Lesson #5
REMAINING STEADFAST IN THE LIGHT
Jesus' fulfillment of Old Testament prophecies

The role of prophecy in the church

The role of prophecy in the individual believer's life

Lesson #6
REJECTING FALSE TEACHING
Recognizing heresy

Responding to heresy

The foremost heresies in the world today

Dealing with false teachers in the church

Lesson #7

LOOKING FOR CHRIST'S COMING

The return of Christ Jesus (the Second Coming)

Time, from God's perspective of eternity

God's longsuffering mercy

God's ultimate judgment of His creation

.

NOTES

NOTES